George Orwell's Animal Farm

Adapted as a Play for the classroom

by Steven Raine

Teacher,

This play is a good starting point for those students learning English as a foreign language and who may want to go on to read George Orwell's novella, *Animal Farm*. This play faithfully preserves all of the narrative's key ideas. The play format allows for participation and focuses on ideas.

I have not included some of the more obscure vernacular references from the original because students learning EFL students would find that language difficult to access. Although students from English native speaking countries would be able to deduce the meaning of vernacular language through context clues, this is not always true for students learning English as a foreign language. The teacher would end up explaining the explanation which in turn would need explaining, and the aim here is to allow students to quickly understand Orwell's intentions.

Each of the five acts, in the play, has separate study questions which would form the basis of five complete lessons. The study questions are derived from international English examinations depending on the level of students.

- KS3 CAMBRIDGE & iGCSE EXAMINATION QUESTIONS
- IELTS & TOEFL TEST QUESTIONS
- SAT TEST & 'A' LEVEL LITERATURE ESSAY QUESTIONS

INDEX

Act One: Old Major — pages 6 - 33

Act Two: The Battle of the Cowshed — pages 34 - 49

Act Three: Long live Comrade Napoleon! — pages 50 - 62

Act Four: Boxer — pages 63 - 72

Act Five: Four Legs Good: Two Legs Better — pages 73 - 92

QUESTIONS FROM INTERNATIONAL EXAMINATIONS

KS3 CAMBRIDGE EXAMINATION & iGCSE QUESTIONS

- Act One: KS3 Study Questions — pages 93 - 97
- Act Two: KS3 Study Questions — pages 98 - 102
- Act Three: KS3 Study Questions — pages 103 - 106
- Act Four: iGCSE Study Questions — pages 107 - 109
- Act Five: iGCSE Study Questions — pages 110 - 113

IELTS & TOEFL TEST QUESTIONS

- IELTS Reading Study Questions — pages 114 - 117
- Act One: IELTS Study Questions — pages 118 - 122
- Act Two: IELTS Study Questions — pages 123 - 126
- Act Three: TOEFL Study — pages 127 – 129
- Act Four: TOEFL Study — pages 130 - 134
- Act Five: TOEFL Study Questions — pages 135 - 137

SAT TEST & 'A' LEVEL LITERATURE EXAMINATION QUESTIONS

- Act One: SAT Study Questions   pages 138 - 140
- Act Two: SAT Study Questions   pages 141 - 145
- Act Three: SAT Study Questions   pages 146 - 151
- Act Four: SAT Study Questions   pages 152 – 155
- Act Five: SAT Study Questions   pages 156 – 161
- 'A' level Essay Questions   pages 162 - 165

Background to Animal Farm

Animal Farm is the story of Farmer Jones and the animals who rebelled against him. Orwell's "Fairy Tale" is an allegory about Communism under Josef Stalin.

At the beginning of the 20th Century, Czar Nicholas II and the Russian ruling class lived in luxury, but ordinary people were poor and worked for the wealthy few. By 1917 this suffering led to angry protests. Czar Nicholas II was forced to abdicate. He and his family were later executed. The Bolshevik Party, under Vladimir Lenin, took control. Russia was renamed the Soviet Union. On Lenin's death (1924), Stalin became the leader. The early idealism of the revolution turned into a terrifying reality. Stalin used the secret police and the military to put down all opposition.

- **Allegory** (aller- gree) A story using one thing to stand in for another. Animal Farm represents real people and events.
- **Bolshevik** (Boll-sha-vick) Political party based on the ideas of Karl Marx (see Marxism)
- **Communism** (kom-you-nizm) All property is owned by the people and each is paid only according to their needs.
- **Idealism** (ideal – izm) To see things as they should be, rather than as they are.
- **Josef Stalin** (Yo-zeff Shtar-leen) Leader of the Soviet Union.
- **Vladimir Lenin** (as written) Russian revolutionary, politician, and first leader of the Communist party.

ACT 1

Old Major

ACT ONE: CHARACTERS

1. NARRATOR (1-3)
2. OLD MAJOR (HOG)
3. CLOVER (HORSE)
4. BLUEBELL (DOG)
5. PINCHER (DOG)
6. MURIEL (GOAT)
7. COW
8. BOXER (HORSE)
9. BENJAMIN (DONKEY)
10. MOLLIE (HORSE)
11. HEN
12. JESSIE (DOG)
13. GOOSE
14. SNOWBALL (PIG)
15. MOSES (RAVEN)
16. JONES (FARMER)
17. NAPOLEON (PIG)
18. SQUEALER (PIG)
19. SHEEP

NARRATOR 1 Jones was drunk.

OLD MAJOR (HOG) I have something to say.

NARRATOR 2 Jones, the farmer, staggered through the front door of the farmhouse and fell flat on his face.

CLOVER (HORSE) Major wants to speak!

BLUEBELL (DOG) Major will speak!

PINCHER (DOG) Tell everyone!

MURIEL (GOAT) Wait until Jones goes to bed and turns off the bedroom light.

COW Listen to his wife snore.

BOXER (HORSE) Look! Jones has left the barn unlocked.

BENJAMIN (DONKEY) Everyone should go to the barn.

NARRATOR 2   Those animals wanting to avoid the intoxicated attentions of Jones, quietly crept into the barn, making themselves as comfortable as fur, feathers, hooves, and horns would allow.

NARRATOR 3   Old Major, the majestic old hog, was highly regarded by the animals, and there was a respectful silence as they waited for Old Major to speak.

NARRATOR 1   Not wanting to interrupt Old Major, the three dogs, Bluebell, Jessie, and Pincher settled silently in the straw.

NARRATOR 2   The two cart-horses, Boxer and Clover, came in together, walking slowly and setting down their vast hairy hoofs with great care, so as not to harm any small animal concealed in the straw.

OLD MAJOR (HOG)   Comrades, I shall not be with you much longer.

MURIEL (GOAT)   NO!

BENJAMIN (DONKEY)   Don't say that, Major!

MOLLIE (HORSE)   Is he leaving the farm?

CLOVER (HORSE)   He thinks he will die soon.

OLD MAJOR (HOG)   Thank you, but I will be free soon. I have had a long life. I have had much time to think.

NARRATOR 3   The pigeons fluttered down to the lower rafters to get a better view.

OLD MAJOR (HOG)   On this farm, the life of an animal is misery and slavery. We are born, given just enough food to keep us breathing, then killed with cruelty when Jones decides we are no longer any use to him.

NARRATOR 1 The hens, perching on the window sills, nodded in agreement.

OLD MAJOR (HOG) Here, no animal is free. Jones destroys families, consumes without producing, withholds food, kills the weak, and prevents us from even owning our own bodies with humiliating rings in our noses, harnesses, bits, spurs, and the whip.

NARRATOR 2 The sheep and cows stopped chewing the cud.

NARRATOR 3 Moses, the raven, squawked.

PINCHER (DOG) MAN IS THE ENEMY!

CLOVER (HORSE) Keep your voice down.

NARRATOR 1 Mollie, the foolish, pretty white mare was chewing a lump of sugar. She had placed herself near the front and began flicking her white mane from side to side, hoping to draw attention to the red ribbons she was wearing.

BLUEBELL(DOG) Humans take everything.

COW They give no milk.

OLD MAJOR (HOG) But they take your milk; the milk that would have fed your young calves.

HEN They lay no eggs.

OLD MAJOR (HOG) ...and how many eggs have you lost? How many should have hatched into chickens?

BOXER (HORSE) Humans are too weak to pull a plow

BLUEBELL(DOG) Too drunk, you mean.

JESSIE (DOG) Can't even run to catch a rabbit.

OLD MAJOR (HOG) And you, Clover, where are your four young foals?

CLOVER (HORSE) He took them...he took them all... sold them at one year old – I will never see my foals again.

OLD MAJOR (HOG) Boxer, he will sell you too! On the day those great muscles of yours lose their power, Jones will sell you to the butcher.

BOXER (HORSE)   Humans!

BENJAMIN (DONKEY)   Only animals are our comrades.

NARRATOR 3   Molly the horse struggled to take it seriously.

MOLLIE (HORSE)   Even rats? Are they our comrades too?

OLD MAJOR (HOG) Then let's put it to a vote. Are rats our comrades?

NARRATOR 1   The vote was taken. Rats were to be comrades too.

OLD MAJOR (HOG) Why is our life miserable? Is it because we are stupid? Is it because humans are superior? Is it because this farm is poor? This farm could support a dozen horses, twenty cows, and hundreds of sheep—all living in comfort and dignity.

NARRATOR 2   Jones, his blood-red face pressed hard into the floor, where he fell, saliva dripping from his mouth, opened one eye.

OLD MAJOR (HOG) The reason is simple. All we produce, all our labor is stolen from us by Jones.

BOXER (HORSE) What must we do?

HEN Drive Jones out!

OLD MAJOR (HOG) Comrades, all our problems can be summed up in a single word — Man.

Man serves the interests of no creature but himself.

Man is the only real enemy we have.

Remove Man and the causes of our hunger and overwork are abolished forever.

HEN Drive Jones out of his house! No animal must ever live in that house.

BLUEBELL (DOG) or...or... sleep in their bed. No animal should sleep in a bed.

HEN What's a bed?

COW	I'll explain later.
JESSIE (DOG)	No animal should wear clothes.
PINCHER (DOG)	...or drink alcohol,
CLOVER (HORSE)	...or touch money,
BOXER (HORSE)	...or sell our food away.
PINCHER (DOG)	KILL JONES!
OLD MAJOR (HOG)	All animals are equal.
BOXER (HORSE)	No animal must ever kill another animal.
NARRATOR 2	As quietly as was possible, for animals, cows mooed, dogs barked, sheep bleated, and horses whinnied. All agreed; no animal must kill another animal.
NARRATOR 3	Jones, both eyes open, heard the noise... pulled himself upright, and went to get his shotgun.

JESSIE (DOG)   Did you hear that?

BOXER (HORSE)   What?

PINCHER (DOG)   It came from the house.

NARRATOR 2   Jones, blurry-eyed, thinking there was a fox in the yard, fired a sparking shot into the black night. The pellets buried themselves in the wall of the barn and the meeting broke up hurriedly.

BENJAMIN (DONKEY) Jones!

JESSIE (DOG)   Let's get out of here!

NARRATOR 1   Everyone fled back to their sleeping places.

GOOSE   Why is Major not moving? He needs to get out of the barn.

NARRATOR 2   The animals were back in their sleeping places...birds perched; the rest settled in straw. The farm was quiet again apart from the steady drumbeat of anxious hearts.

BOXER (HORSE)   Major, you have to hide. You can't stay here.

OLD MAJOR (HOG) Jones won't harm me. I am too old to sell. He won't kill his prize-winning hog without a profit. You go. I'll rest here for a while.

NARRATOR 3   Two days later, old Major was at rest - forever. He died peacefully in his sleep. His body was buried at the foot of the orchard, but Major's words had given all the animals a new vision of what might be.

BENJAMIN (DONKEY) Is it possible?

COW   No humans?

BENJAMIN (DONKEY) Is it right to take the farm?

SNOWBALL (PIG) It's better to die on our feet than live on our knees.

HEN   Did Major say that?

SNOWBALL (PIG)   No, one of the dogs told me. He read it in a book after Jones had thrown it at his head.

NARRATOR 2 Of the clever pigs and there were a few, Snowball was the cleverest and most popular. It was expected that Snowball would be the natural choice as leader after Old Major.

NARRATOR 3 Snowball, Napoleon, and Squealer, turned old Major's words into a new philosophy. They called this new way of thinking 'Animalism'.

MOLLIE (HORSE) But if Mr. Jones is not here who will feed us? We'll all starve without Jones. There will be no more sugar!

SNOWBALL (PIG) You don't need sugar.

BOXER (HORSE) We'll have all the oats and hay we want.

MOLLIE (HORSE) Oh, I see... but can I still wear ribbons in my mane?

SNOWBALL (PIG) Comrade Mollie, ribbons are the badge of your slavery.

MOSES (RAVEN) Why should we care about this life anyway?

NARRATOR 3 Moses, the raven, who had never worked a day, was Jones' spy. His squawks were warning signals. The animals hated Moses but some loved to hear his comforting stories about animal heaven - some place called Sugarcandy Mountain - in the sky- where all animals went when they died.

MOSES (RAVEN) On Sugarcandy Mountain, it is Sunday every day. Sugar and cake grow on trees.

NARRATOR 1 Jones, once a good farmer until he started drinking more and more, lay unconscious again on the farmhouse kitchen floor.

BLUEBELL (DOG) Is he dead?

JESSIE (DOG) No, just drunk.

PINCHER (DOG)	Quickly, before he wakes up.
JESSIE (DOG)	This time just take food and leave the books and newspapers.
PINCHER (DOG)	But I'm learning to read.
NARRATOR 2	Because Jones was drunk nearly all the time, the fields were weeds, the fences broken and the animals starved.
GOOSE	We're so hungry. Maybe the hens have something we can eat.
NARRATOR 3	One Saturday, Jones was so drunk he did not come back for two days...
MOLLIE (HORSE)	We'll all die!
COW	I'm so hungry.
NARRATOR 1	The animals could stand it no longer. The cow broke down the door of the storeroom.
MURIEL (GOAT)	Quick! before the pigs take it all.

NARRATOR 2 All animals, except Moses the Raven, began to feed themselves.

NARRATOR 3 Jones could hardly stand let alone run, but he managed to follow Moses to the storeroom with his whip, lashing out in all directions.

JONES (FARMER) I'll send you all to the butcher.

NARRATOR 1 Famished and ravenous eyes glared at Mr. Jones. Hatred filled their hearts. Moses flew away. Jones was not sure what to do. All animals flung themselves at him, butting, scratching, biting, and kicking.

NARRATOR 2 Jones ran for his life.

BOXER (HORSE) After him!

BENJAMIN (DONKEY) Leave him.

CLOVER (HORSE) But he's getting away.

NARRATOR 3	Mrs. Jones scooped up everything within reach and hurled it into a small suitcase, slipping out of the back door. The cow, hens, and a goose watched.
COW	Fast for a human.
HEN	They can move when they want to.
GOOSE	I suppose they'll be back.
HEN	Yes, but not today.
NARRATOR 1	Moses flapped and croaked flying above but never behind his master.
GOOSE	There goes, Moses.
HEN	He'll be back. Moses always comes back.
NARRATOR 2	The Farm was theirs. It belonged to the animals. All traces of Jones's rule were to be removed.
MURIEL (GOAT)	Build a fire.

SNOWBALL (PIG)   Let's burn everything that will remind us of our slavery.

NARRATOR 2   The harness room was the first to be broken open.

BOXER (HORSE)   Get the nose rings, dog chains, and knives, and throw them on the fire.

BENJAMIN (DONKEY)   Burn the whips and sticks he uses to beat us.

GOOSE   Burn it all.

NAPOLEON (PIG)   STOP!

MOLLIE (HORSE)   Napoleon?

CLOVER (HORSE)   Yes, that's Napoleon?

BLUEBELL (DOG)   I know.

BENJAMIN (DONKEY)   He never comes outside.

JESSIE (DOG)   We know Napoleon.

BLUEBELL (DOG)   He took our puppies

JESSIE (DOG)   We gave him our puppies.

BOXER (HORSE) — Why did you give him your puppies?

BLUEBELL (DOG) — Jones wouldn't let us keep them.

JESSIE (DOG) — Jones was going to take them to the village.

BLUEBELL (DOG) — ...or worse.

JESSIE (DOG) — Napoleon said he would look after them.

BLUEBELL (DOG) — Hide them, feed them, at least that way I could see them.

JESSIE (DOG) — That's what he promised.

BLUEBELL (DOG) — We never saw our puppies again.

NARRATOR 3 — Napoleon led all animals to Jones' house. The animals nervously peeked through the windows as if they still expected to see Jones.

BOXER (HORSE) — I've never been this close to the house before.

CLOVER (HORSE)　　Move, let me see.

MOLLIE (HORSE)　　What can you see?

NARRATOR 1　　Napoleon nodded to Snowball who then head-butted the front door open.

MOLLIE (HORSE) –(*SCREAM*)…. sorry.

NARRATOR 2　　Afraid to speak, each animal explored room after room, amazed at the luxury they saw.

MURIEL (GOAT)　　Look at the beds with feather mattresses.

COW　　What's a bed?

BLUEBELL　　I'll explain later.

BOXER (HORSE)　　The mirrors -the sofa-the carpets.

MOLLIE (HORSE)　　Look at these beautiful ribbons. Can I take one? Can I take one, please?

NARRATOR 3　　A resolution was passed; the farmhouse would be preserved as a museum for future generations.

SNOWBALL (PIG)   Comrades, we have a long day before us. Today we must begin gathering in the harvest, our harvest.

NAPOLEON (PIG)   Snowball, you can read and write. Get paint and go to the gate. Paint out MANOR FARM, and paint on ANIMAL FARM.

NARRATOR 2   ...and on the barn door, now regarded as a holy place because it was where Major had spoken for the last time, they painted,

'THE SEVEN COMMANDMENTS'.

SNOWBALL (PIG)   1. WHATEVER GOES UPON TWO LEGS IS AN ENEMY.

NARRATOR 3   The birds objected since it seemed to them that they also had two legs, but Snowball proved to them that this was not so.

SNOWBALL (PIG) A bird's wing, comrades, is an organ of propulsion and not of manipulation. It should therefore be regarded as a leg. The distinguishing mark of man is the hand, the instrument with which he does all his evil.

NARRATOR 1 The birds did not understand Snowball's long words, but they accepted his explanation.

SNOWBALL (PIG) 2. WHATEVER GOES UPON FOUR LEGS…OR HAS WINGS…IS A FRIEND.   3.NO ANIMAL SHALL WEAR CLOTHES.

MOLLIE (HORSE) Are ribbons clothes?

SNOWBALL (PIG) 4.NO ANIMAL SHALL SLEEP IN A BED.

COW What's a bed?

BLUEBELL (DOG) … later.

SNOWBALL (PIG)   5. NO ANIMAL SHALL DRINK ALCOHOL.
6. NO ANIMAL SHALL KILL ANY OTHER ANIMAL.
7. ALL ANIMALS ARE EQUAL.

NARRATOR 3   All cheered. Horses whinnied, sheep and goats bleated, the raven squawked, donkeys brayed, dogs barked, geese honked, pigs grunted, hens clucked, and pigeons cooed.

COW   That's all very well, but I have not been milked for a whole day, and my udders are bursting.

NAPOLEON (PIG)   Get buckets and milk the cows.

COW   What is going to happen to all that milk?

HEN   Jones usually used it to mix in our mash.

NAPOLEON (PIG)   Never mind the milk. The harvest is more important. Forward, comrades!

NARRATOR 3 The animals happily marched to the hayfield to begin the harvest that was for animals alone. They chanted as they marched.

BOXER (HORSE) HUMANS ARE WEAK.

CLOVER (HORSE) ANIMALS ARE EQUAL

BLUEBELL (DOG) HUMANS PRODUCE NOTHING

COW HUMANS GIVE NO MILK

HEN HUMANS LAY NO EGGS

PINCHER (DOG) MAN IS THE ENEMY!

MURIEL (GOAT) FOUR IS GOOD; TWO IS BAD.

BENJAMIN (DONKEY) ANIMALS ARE OUR COMRADES

JESSIE (DOG) THE FARM BELONGS TO US!

NARRATOR 1 When they came back in the evening, exhausted but content, all the milk had gone. Squealer's eyes darted from one disbelieving animal to another. He distracted them with his new flag.

SQUEALER (PIG)   I've made a flag from the green tablecloth in the kitchen, and painted a hoof and horn, in white. This will be our flag.

MOLLIE (HORSE)   It's beautiful.

SNOWBALL (PIG)   Are you happy now   Jones has gone?

BENJAMIN (DONKEY)   Humans and most animals come and go, but donkeys, live a long time. I bet none of you has seen a dead donkey.

NARRATOR 2   Everyone had stopped asking Benjamin what he meant when he spoke like that.

NARRATOR 1   The pigs did no work; they supervised and stood behind the horses shouting orders.

BOXER (HORSE)   We will make this work. I will work harder. I have made an arrangement with the cockerel to wake me early in the morning. is right.

SHEEP Work harder.

BOXER (HORSE) In the evenings, when I get back, I want to learn more letters of the alphabet. I am up to 'D' already.

NARRATOR 2 The clever pigs studied metalwork, and carpentry.

SNOWBALL (PIG) I have formed the Egg Production Committee for hens, the Wild Comrades' Re-education Committee for rats and rabbits, and the Clean Tails League. There will be classes for reading and writing.

NAPOLEON (PIG) These projects of yours, Snowball, they're pointless. This reading and writing class? Mollie, the horse, won't learn more than the six letters in her own name. Boxer can't get passed four letters. The stupid sheep and hens can't even learn the Seven Commandments.

SNOWBALL (PIG)   Then we'll make the Seven Commandments easier to learn.

SQUEALER (PIG)   Four legs good, two legs bad!

SHEEP   Four legs good, two legs bad! Four legs good, two legs bad!

NARRATOR 3   If the sheep had been better educated, they might have realized that Squealer was taking advantage of them. But for now, their focus was on the apples which were finally ripe, and the animals looked forward to sharing them equally.

SQUEALER (PIG)   All apples are to be brought to us pigs.

NARRATOR 1   Along with the new apple policy, the mystery of the missing milk was also solved. It had been mixed every day into the pigs' food.

NAPOLEON   Squealer, you're good at talking. Explain it to them.

SQUEALER (PIG)   Comrades! Comrades! The truth is, we pigs are not selfish. We don't even like milk or apples, but the management of this farm depends on us. We drink milk and eat apples for you. It is our sacrifice for you. If we pigs fail in our duty, Jones will come back! Is that what you all want? Do you want Jones back?

GOOSE   Isn't the food for all of us, equally?

NARRATOR 2   Squealer ignored the question and looked up into the sky where the pigeons had been ordered to fly to all the neighboring farms with the story of the rebellion.

SHEEP   Four legs good, two legs bad!

ACT 2
The Battle of the Cowshed

ACT TWO: CHARACTERS

1. NARRATOR (1-3)
2. SHEEP
3. JONES (FARMER)
4. PIGEONS
5. SNOWBALL (PIG)
6. BOXER (HORSE)
7. GOOSE
8. NAPOLEON (PIG)
9. SQUEALER (Pig)
10. MOLLIE (HORSE)
11. MURIEL (GOAT)
12. CLOVER (Horse)
13. HEN
14. COW
15. BLUEBELL (DOG)
16. PINCHER (DOG)

NARRATOR 1 Rebellion was in the air. Animals all over the countryside protested. Bulls turned savage, sheep broke fences, cows kicked buckets, and horses threw humans off their backs.

SHEEP Four legs good, two legs bad!

NARRATOR 3 Jones, was drinking heavily.

NARRATOR 1 The local farmers, now gathered around Mr. Jones in the Red Lion pub, had no interest in Jones' drunken self-pity but were interested in his failing farm which they had hoped to buy at a bargain price.

NARRATOR 2 The idea that animals could successfully run Jones' farm was alarming.

JONES (FARMER) It's unnatural, against nature, animals running a farm. There'll be torture, I'm telling you, torture with red-hot horseshoes. They'll all starve to death. They'll all become cannibals.

NARRATOR 1   But, to the annoyance of Jones the animals did not starve. He would have to act.

PIGEONS   QUICK! LOOK! IT'S JONES AND OTHER HUMANS. THEY'RE COMING DOWN THE ROAD! JONES, HAS A GUN.

NARRATOR 2   Snowball, calm in the swirls of churning dust kicked up by panicking hooves, had been expecting this. He'd studied an old book on Julius Caesar which he'd found in the farmhouse. He gave his orders.

SNOWBALL (PIG)   Muriel, Benjamin, and the sheep, follow me!

NARRATOR 3   Pigeons flew over the men's heads, their droppings pounding down. The geese, behind the hedge, rushed out and pecked hard at legs and ankles.

NARRATOR 1   They all rushed forward, prodding and butting.

SNOWBALL (PIG)   Fall back! Fall back!

NARRATOR 2   The men had sticks and boots and were too strong,

SNOWBALL (PIG)   Back! Back to the farmyard.

NARRATOR 3   The men shouted in triumph, rushing after the animals, just as Snowball had predicted they would.

SNOWBALL (PIG)   Horses and cows stand ready!

NARRATOR 2   As soon as the humans were inside the yard, the horses and cows rushed out from their hiding places.

SNOWBALL (PIG)   ATTACK! ATTACK! I'll take care of Jones.

NARRATOR 1   But, Jones saw Snowball coming, raised his gun, and fired. The pellets scored bloody streaks along Snowball's back, and one of the sheep was killed.

SNOWBALL (PIG)   Leave Jones: he's mine.

NARRATOR 3 Snowball flung his full weight against Jones, hurling him into a pile of dung.

NARRATOR 2 Boxer, reared up on his hind legs, striking down with his heavy iron hoofs, hitting a stable lad on the skull-his lifeless body stretched out in the mud.

BOXER (HORSE) Is the boy dead? I didn't want to hurt anyone. I forgot I was wearing iron shoes. Please believe me. I didn't do this on purpose?

NARRATOR 1 The men dropped their sticks and ran. All the animals chased after them-growling and barking, gouging and kicking, biting and head-butting.

SNOWBALL (PIG) Boxer, war is war.

NAPOLEON (PIG) The only good human is a dead one.

BOXER (HORSE) I have no wish to take life, not even human life.

SNOWBALL (PIG) Look over there. You haven't killed anyone. The stable lad was only stunned.

NARRATOR 2 The boy ran off down the main road before anyone could stop him.

SNOWBALL (PIG) Get Jones' gun, and the spare bullets from the farmhouse; we'll put it by the flagstaff in the middle of the farmyard. We will fire the gun on every anniversary of this battle.

GOOSE Battle of the Cowshed

NARRATOR 3 Everyone agreed that it was to be called, The Battle of the Cowshed. The flag was raised and the dead sheep was given a solemn funeral.

NARRATOR 1 Military decorations were created.

NAPOLEON (PIG) I award "Animal Hero, First Class," to Snowball and Boxer – and "Animal Hero, Second Class," to the dead sheep.

NARRATOR 2 All cheered. Horses whinnied, sheep and goats bleated, the raven squawked, donkeys brayed, dogs barked, geese honked, pigs grunted, hens clucked, and pigeons cooed.

NARRATOR 3 Even as all the animals were celebrating their victory, Napoleon and Squealer slowly pushed Mollie into a quiet corner of the farmyard.

SQUEALER (Pig) Mollie, this morning we saw you talking to one of the men from the farm next door.

NAPOLEON (PIG) You were allowing the human to stroke you.

MOLLIE (HORSE) He didn't! I wasn't! It isn't true!

NAPOLEON (PIG) Mollie! Look at me! Look me in the face.

MOLLIE (HORSE) It isn't true!

SQUEALER (PIG) We saw you with that man.

NAPOLEON (PIG) You let him feed you sugar.

MOLLIE (HORSE) Please! It isn't true!

NARRATOR 1 As winter drew on, Mollie became more and more troublesome. She was late for work every morning and excused herself by saying that she had overslept, or complaining of mysterious pains, although her appetite was, obviously, excellent.

MURIEL (GOAT) She likes to go to the drinking pool, and gaze at her own reflection.

NARRATOR 3 No one knew exactly when, but Mollie had disappeared from the farm.

NARRATOR 2 Later, the pigeons saw Mollie by the village pub, the Landlord feeding her sugar, she wore a red ribbon in her mane. None of the animals were allowed to mention Mollie again.

NARRATOR 3 The winter was harsh, food scarce, and arguments between Snowball and Napoleon grew more bitter.

SHEEP Four legs good, two legs bad.

NARRATOR 2 Snowball wanted to build a windmill.

SNOWBALL (Pig) The power will light and warm the stalls -work the milking machine.

NAPOLEON (Pig) We need food not windmills

SNOWBALL (Pig) Electricity will operate machines, and supply every stall with light, hot and cold water, and an electric heater.

NARRATOR 3 The animals started to gather around Snowball. They wanted to hear more.

BOXER (HORSE) I will help you build your electric wind drill.

NARRATOR 1 Napoleon and Squealer stepped out of the crowd of animals unnoticed. They found a quiet corner in the yard and whispered.

SNOWBALL (Pig) It's called a wind mill and it will make electricity. I know just the place to build it: near the pasture.

BOXER (HORSE)   When I retire up to the pasture, I will guard our windmill.

SNOWBALL (Pig)   The windmill will have a dynamo and supply the farm with electricity.

CLOVER (Horse)   We can have lights in our stalls like Jones had in his house

HEN   And electric heaters to keep us warm in winter . . .

NARRATOR 2   The animals listened in astonishment while Snowball conjured up pictures of fantastic machines which would do their work for them while they grazed in the high pasture grass.

BOXER (HORSE)   With machines doing the work, I will have time to improve my reading and conversation.

NARRATOR 3   Napoleon interrupted.

NAPOLEON (PIG)   Of course, we will need money for materials. I will make arrangements to sell hay and wheat, and later on, if more money is needed, sell eggs.

HEN   Didn't we say no engaging in trade?

NARRATOR 1   Napoleon cared nothing for the windmill and later would urinate on Snowball's plans for it.

He whispered to Squealer.

NAPOLEON (PIG)   If the windmill is successful, and the animals have their workload decreased, they will be able to relax.

SQUEALER (PIG)   …and blame us for everything.

NAPOLEON (PIG)   …They'll want Snowball to be the leader.

SQUEALER (PIG)   No windmill?

NAPOLEON (PIG)   No windmill! We need them overworked and exhausted so they can't think about things they shouldn't be thinking about.

SQUEALER (PIG)   But...

NARRATOR 2   Squealer felt bold enough to say it but wise enough to step back from Napoleon.

NAPOLEON (PIG)   But WHAT?

SQUEALER (PIG)   The windmill was your idea.

NAPOLEON (PIG)   Was it?

SQUEALER (PIG)   Snowball stole your idea.

NAPOLEON (PIG)   Did he?

SQUEALER (PIG)   You said the animals need a project, something that gives them responsibility, keeps them busy...

NAPOLEON (PIG)   ...A windmill?

SQUEALER (PIG)   Why not? It's a project. Building a windmill will keep them busy. We just make sure the windmill never works or is never finished.

NAPOLEON (PIG)   Yes, that was my idea, wasn't it?

NARRATOR 3   Squealer told Snowball that Napoleon wanted to meet with him in the barn; to discuss his excellent idea about the windmill.

SNOWBALL (PIG)   Does he? Does Napoleon like it? I am so happy. You'll see. It will change everything.

NARRATOR 1   When Snowball entered the barn, Napoleon was waiting for him. In an impressive imitation of anger, Napoleon let loose a high-pitched squeal.

SNOWBALL (PIG)   What's wrong? What's going on?

NARRATOR 3 At the same moment, a terrible howling, as nine enormous dogs wearing brass-studded collars came bounding into the barn. They dashed straight for Snowball, who only escaped because their snapping jaws couldn't get a biting grip on his plump pig pink body.

NARRATOR 2 Snowball raced out and away across the fields.

BOXER (HORSE) Why is Snowball running?

CLOVER (HORSE) I heard dogs!

COW Maybe we should go and see what has happened in the barn?

NARRATOR 1 The rest of the animals were too frightened to find out what was going on in the barn.

Bluebell the dog had her head down.

MURIEL (GOAT)   Where did those dogs come from?

BLUEBELL (DOG)   My puppies!

PINCHER (DOG)   Now we know why he wanted our puppies.

NARRATOR 1   As fierce-looking as wolves, the dogs always stayed close to Napoleon. They trotted out of the barn behind him, wagging their tails. Then Napoleon stopped and looked with contempt at all the animals gathered in the farmyard

NAPOLEON (PIG)   These meetings you like to have in the yard will have to end. Talking together like that. All animals will gather every week to salute the flag, but no more ideas. No more talking. Leave the thinking to us.

SHEEP   Four legs good, two legs bad!

ACT 3
Long live Comrade Napoleon!

ACT THREE: CHARACTERS

1. SQUEALER (PIG)
2. NARRATOR (S)
3. BOXER (HORSE)
4. BENJAMIN (DONKEY)
5. NAPOLEON (PIG)
6. PINCHER (DOG)
7. CLOVER (HORSE)
8. SHEEP
9. MINIMUS (PIG)
10. HEN
11. GOOSE
12. MINIMUS (PIG)
13. MURIEL (GOAT)
14. COW
15. BLUEBELL (DOG)
16. JESSIE(DOG)
17. MOSES (RAVEN)

SQUEALER (PIG)   Comrades! Comrades!

NARRATOR 2   Squealer put on his soft voice.

SQUEALER (PIG)   You see, it's like this. Leadership is a heavy responsibility. Comrade Napoleon believes all animals are equal, but sometimes…well sometimes… you might have the wrong idea. Snowball has run off to join the humans. Snowball is a traitor and a criminal.

BOXER (HORSE)   But Snowball fought bravely at the Battle of the Cowshed.

SQUEALER (PIG)   Snowball's part in the Battle of the Cowshed was much exaggerated

BENJAMIN (DONKEY)   We awarded him 'Animal Hero, First Class,'?

SQUEALER (PIG)   Comrades! Loyalty and obedience are more important. One false step and our enemies will be upon us! Surely, comrades, you don't want Jones back!

BOXER (HORSE)   If Comrade Napoleon says it is right, it must be right. Napoleon is always right; I will work harder. We must all work harder.

NARRATOR 1   Napoleon stepped out from behind Squealer to make an announcement.

NAPOLEON (PIG)   The windmill will be built in two years. This task will mean hard work. We may need to reduce rations.

SQUEALER (PIG)   You see comrades, Snowball had stolen the idea of the Windmill from Napoleon...

PINCHER (DOG)   Why did Napoleon speak so strongly against it then?

SQUEALER (PIG)   Comrade. Napoleon is clever. He had pretended to oppose the windmill, to get rid of Snowball, who was dangerous to us all. Now that Snowball is gone, the plan can go forward

NAPOLEON (PIG)   Oh, and from now on Animal Farm will trade with the other farms.

CLOVER (HORSE)   Didn't we all decide we would never trade with humans, never use money?

SQUEALER (PIG)   Have you any record of such a decision? Is it written down?"

SHEEP   Four legs good, two legs bad!

NAPOLEON (PIG)   I will take the whole burden of trade on my shoulders. Mr. Whimper, a lawyer in the village, has agreed to represent Animal Farm. He will visit every Monday morning to receive his instructions from me.

SHEEP   Long live Animal Farm!

NARRATOR 2   The animals, with heads lowered, started to leave the yard.

NAPOLEON (PIG)   Wait! Comrade Minimus has a poem.

NARRATOR 3 The animals looked at each other and reluctantly turned around. Using his snout, Napoleon nudged a small pig forward. The small pig coughed to clear his throat

MINIMUS (PIG) COMRADE NAPOLEON…

That's what the poem's called.

Comrade Napoleon. Friend of the fatherless! Fountain of happiness! Lord of the swill-bucket! Oh, how my soul is on Fire when I gaze at thy Calm and commanding eye, Like the sun in the sky, Comrade Napoleon!

NARRATOR 2 There was a long silence.

BENJAMIN (DONKEY) It's terrible

NARRATOR 3 Clover kicked Benjamin.

BENJAMIN (DONKEY) It's terribly good.

MINIMUS (PIG)　　　　　Really?

CLOVER (HORSE)　　　　…and clever

HEN　　　　　　　　　　Yes, clever

GOOSE　　　　　　　　Oh yes, very clever

MINIMUS (PIG)　　　　　Why?

BOXER (HORSE)　　　　Why what?

MINIMUS (PIG)　　　　　Why is it clever?

MURIEL (GOAT)　　　　Why is it clever?　Well…. For example…how you rhyme the words eye with sky

COW　　　　　　　　　Yes, that is clever, but not as clever as the rhyme fatherless and happiness.

BLUEBELL (DOG)　　　Impressive.

PINCHER (DOG)　　　　Very impressive.

JESSIE(DOG)　　　　　Lord of the swill-bucket!

BENJAMIN (DONKEY) Yes, bucket, smart.

CLOVER (HORSE)　　　Very smart

HEN	The poem makes us all very happy.
MINIMUS (PIG)	Shall I tell it you again?
BENJAMIN (DONKEY)	No! No! No!
CLOVER (HORSE)	That would make us too happy.
NARRATOR 3	Minimus' little tail swung happily from side to side like a pendulum
NARRATOR 2	Over the coming weeks, the animals watched Mr. Whimper's comings and goings. Indeed, the sight of Napoleon, giving orders to a human, raised their pride, and so they didn't notice when the pigs moved into the farmhouse.
SQUEALER. (PIG)	Comrades, we pigs should have a quiet place to work. It is better for Napoleon, our leader, to be seen, by the humans, living in a house, not a dirty old shed.

BENJAMIN (DONKEY)   The dirty old shed is good enough for us, though.

COW   Someone told me the pigs take their meals in the kitchen and use the drawing room as a games room.

HEN   I was told they sleep in the beds.

MURIEL (GOAT)   When did we decide Napoleon was the leader anyway?

CLOVER (HORSE)   Muriel, none of us can read as well as you. Please read the Fourth Commandment. Does it not say something about never sleeping in beds?

MURIEL (GOAT)   Benjamin can read. He can read as well as any pig

CLOVER (HORSE)   Benjamin, why do you never read

BENJAMIN (DONKEY) Nothing worth reading.

MURIEL (GOAT)   It says, No animal shall sleep in a bed...with sheets.

NARRATOR 3   The words…with sheets… had recently been added.

CLOVER (HORSE)   Are you sure it says with sheets? I don't remember that.

BENJAMIN (DONKEY) Muriel is right. It says with sheets.

CLOVER (HORSE)   Benjamin, if you read, you knew. Why didn't you tell us?

BENJAMIN (DONKEY) I don't meddle in such matters.

MURIEL (GOAT)   It's not the only Commandment they have changed. the Fifth Commandment used to read "No animal shall drink alcohol." Now it reads, "No animal shall drink too much alcohol."

"No animal shall kill any other animal" they've changed that to, "No animal shall kill any other animal without cause."

SQUEALER (PIG)   Comrades, comrades, a bed is just a place to sleep. A pile of straw is a bed. The rule was against sheets not beds. We have removed the sheets.

NARRATOR 1   After the hay and corn were sold, the stores of food for winter were nearly empty, but the windmill was almost half-built.

SQUEALER (PIG)   I'm sorry Comrades. There are no apples left and we are low on grain. We are selling everything we can to get more food, but we will have to cut the rations.

NARRATOR 3   In their spare time, the animals would walk around the half-finished mill, admiring the strength of its walls.

BOXER (HORSE)   It's nearly finished. I'm so proud.

NARRATOR 1   The winter was cold and the food short. All rations were reduced, except for the pigs' rations.

GOOSE	I'm hungry.
CLOVER (HORSE)	We're all hungry.
BENJAMIN (DONKEY)	Not all are hungry. The pigs are not hungry.
JESSIE (DOG)	Snowball would be proud.
BLUEBELL (DOG)	We've all worked hard on this windmill.
PINCHER (DOG)	I miss Snowball. He talked pretty.
MOSES (RAVEN)	You can't talk about Snowball.
BOXER (HORSE)	We are all together. working to finish the windmill. That's important.
MURIEL (GOAT)	You work the hardest, Boxer. But look how sick you are.
HEN	The pigs don't work at all!

BOXER (HORSE)   They work hard in their own way. They are clever. They organize everything. Napoleon is always right.

SHEEP (Chorus)   Long live Animal Farm. Long live Comrade Napoleon!

BENJAMIN (DONKEY)   Muriel's right. You don't look well, Boxer.

NARRATOR 2   The animals got thinner and weaker, except Napoleon and the pigs who got fatter and stronger. Instead of food, there were more songs, more speeches, more processions, and worse of all more poetry.

SHEEP   Long live Comrade Napoleon!

ACT 4
Boxer

ACT FOUR: CHARACTERS

1. NARRATOR(S)
2. MURIEL (GOAT)
3. BENJAMIN (DONKEY)
4. NAPOLEON (PIG)
5. SQUEALER. (PIG)
6. SHEEP
7. PIGEON
8. CLOVER (HORSE)
9. BOXER (HORSE)
10. MOSES (RAVEN)
11. BLUEBELL (DOG)
12. JESSIE(DOG)
13. PINCHER (DOG)

NARRATOR 3 Animal Farm was proclaimed a Republic, with only one candidate for president, Napoleon.

MURIEL (GOAT) Look how thin Boxer is now

BENJAMIN (DONKEY) He'll pick up again when the spring grass comes.

NARRATOR 1 Winter came, with raging winds. But even with the sound of storms and thunder, everyone heard the cry of despair from every animal when they saw the windmill.

The windmill had been destroyed.

NAPOLEON (PIG) Do you know who is responsible for this? Do you know the enemy who has come at night and destroyed our windmill? SNOWBALL!

SQUEALER. (PIG) The traitor has destroyed our work.

NAPOLEON (PIG) I pronounce the death sentence on Snowball...

SQUEALER. (PIG) Two dozen apples to any animal who captures him alive!

MURIEL (GOAT) I thought there were no apples left.

NAPOLEON (PIG) No more delays, comrades! There is work to be done. We must rebuild the windmill. We will teach this traitor that he cannot undo our work so easily.

SHEEP Long live the windmill! Long live Napoleon!"

NARRATOR 2 The spring came but Boxer grew no fatter.

PIGEON COME QUICK! Boxer has fallen! He can't get up!

CLOVER (HORSE) Boxer! how are you? There's blood on your mouth!

BOXER (HORSE)   It is my lung. To tell the truth, I had been looking forward to my retirement. And perhaps, as Benjamin is growing old too, they will let him retire at the same time and be my companion in the pasture.

BENJAMIN (DONKEY)   We must get help. Run, somebody, tell someone.

NARRATOR 1   Benjamin was devoted to Boxer; the two of them usually spent their Sundays together in the small paddock beyond the orchard, grazing side by side and never speaking. Benjamin, lay down at Boxer's side, keeping the flies off with his long tail. Squealer finally arrived.

SQUEALER (PIG)   Napoleon is distressed, comrades. His most loyal worker, "My most loyal worker" he says. I heard him say it. We'll send Boxer to the hospital in the village.

NARRATOR 2 The animals felt uneasy. They did not like to think of their sick friend in the hands of humans.

SQUEALER (PIG) There's a veterinary surgeon in the village. Boxer will be well taken care of.

BENJAMIN (DONKEY) Let's get him back to his stall; make a good bed of straw.

NARRATOR 2 Moses the raven perched above Boxer and squawked.

MOSES (RAVEN) Up there, Boxer, just on the other side of the clouds is Sugarcandy Mountain, that happy country where we poor animals shall rest forever. I have seen it. I flew so high once I saw it myself. Everlasting fields of grass. Cake and sugar growing on trees.

BOXER (HORSE) Get away Moses. I'm not dying yet. I can live another three years, peaceful days on the big pasture. Perhaps I will have time to study? I could learn the other letters of the alphabet.

NARRATOR 2 The following day Benjamin came galloping up to the fields from the farm.

BENJAMIN (DONKEY) QUICK, QUICK! COME NOW! THEY'RE TAKING BOXER AWAY!

NARRATOR 3 There, in the yard, was a large van drawn by two horses, with lettering on its side. Boxer's stall was empty. The animals crowded around the van.

MURIEL (GOAT) Goodbye, Boxer!

SQUEALER (PIG) Goodbye!

BENJAMIN (DONKEY) Fools! Don't you see what is written on that van?"

NARRATOR 1 Muriel began to spell out the words, but Benjamin pushed her aside impatiently.

BENJAMIN (DONKEY) It says, 'Horse Slaughterer, and Dog Food Supplier.' Do you not understand? They are taking Boxer to be killed!

NARRATOR 2 A cry of horror burst from all the animals. The van moved, and the animals followed, crying out.

CLOVER (HORSE) Boxer! Boxer!

NARRATOR 3 Boxer's face appeared in the small window at the back of the van.

BENJAMIN (DONKEY) Get out! Get out quickly! They're taking you to your death!"

NARRATOR 1 But the van went faster. There was tremendous drumming of hoofs inside the van. Boxer was trying to kick his way out, but his strength had left him.

NARRATOR 2 Benjamin tried to appeal to the two horses pulling the van.

BENJAMIN (DONKEY) Comrades, don't take your brother to his death!

CLOVER (HORSE) It's no use, Benjamin. They're just stupid brutes, too ignorant to realize what they do.

NARRATOR 3	Three days later it was announced that Boxer had died in the hospital.
SQUEALER (PIG)	Comrades, I was there during Boxer's last hours…
NARRATOR 1	Squealer lifted his trotter and wiped away a tear.
SQUEALER (PIG)	I was at his bedside. He whispered in my ear. "Forward, comrades. Long live Animal Farm! Long live Comrade Napoleon! Napoleon is always right." Those were his very last words, comrades.
NARRATOR 2	Squealer's black eyes darted suspiciously at each unbelieving animal.
SQUEALER (PIG)	There is a wicked rumor that the van was marked "Horse Slaughterer,". The explanation is simple comrades. The van was the property of the "Horse Slaughterer' but had been bought by the hospital, they just forgot to paint the old name out.

NARRATOR 3 A van drove up from the village delivering a large wooden crate to the farmhouse. At night there was the sound of loud singing.

BLUEBELL (DOG) They're drunk.

JESSIE (DOG) They bought a crate of whiskey.

PINCHER (DOG) With what? They said there was no money

BENJAMIN (DONKEY) What money, from where?

NARRATOR 3 The animals knew where the money was from. They turned their heads away.

MURIEL (GOAT) There was never going to be a peaceful retirement up on the pasture for Boxer…quiet evenings learning the alphabet…THERE WAS NO HOSPITAL! THEY SOLD BOXER TO THE BUTCHER, FOR WHISKEY.

ACT 5

Four Legs Good
Two Legs Better

ACT FIVE: CHARACTERS

1. NARRATOR(S)
2. MINIMUS (PIG)
3. JESSIE (DOG)
4. PINCHER (DOG)
5. COW
6. BLUEBELL (DOG)
7. PINCHER (DOG)
8. SQUEALER (PIG)
9. HENS
10. CLOVER (HORSE)
11. BENJAMIN (DONKEY)
12. MURIEL (GOAT)
13. PIGEON
14. NAPOLEON (PIG)
15. GEESE
16. HEN

NARRATOR 1 When the old ones remembered these times, they did so in whispers for what happened next was unbelievable.

NARRATOR 2 It began in January when the corn ration was reduced, again, and they had to listen to another poem by Comrade Minimus.

MINIMUS (PIG) Thou art the giver of all that thy creatures love, Full belly twice a day, clean straw to roll upon; every beast, great or small, sleeps at peace in his stall, thou watch over all, Comrade Napoleon!

JESSIE(DOG) It's even more unbelievable than the last one.

MINIMUS (PIG) Unbelievable?

PINCHER (DOG) She means masterpiece…It's a masterpiece.

MINIMUS (PIG) Oh, it's not that good.

COW It's not good.

MINIMUS (PIG) It's not?

BLUEBELL (DOG)   It's beyond good. It may be the greatest poem ever written.

JESSIE (DOG)   Has anyone seen the geese?

NARRATOR 3   The disappearances had begun.

PINCHER (DOG)   Some hens have gone too?

NARRATOR 1   First to vanish were three hens and all the geese.

COW   Maybe they've just left the farm like Mollie and Snowball?

BLUEBELL (DOG)   ...or maybe they left like Boxer?

NARRATOR 2   Napoleon, who rarely appeared outside the farmhouse and was guarded by his dogs, told Squealer to explain.

SQUEALER (PIG)   Dear Comrades, the hens must surrender their eggs. The leader has arranged to sell the eggs to pay for grain and keep the farm going.

HENS   We will not! We will smash our eggs before we give them up.

NARRATOR 3	Napoleon ordered the hens' rations to be stopped. Four hens died, but once a week, a grocer's van drove up to the farm to take the eggs.
CLOVER (HORSE)	We have to stop them,
BENJAMIN (DONKEY)	Stop who?
MURIEL (GOAT)	Stop them taking the eggs.
PIGEON	Napoleon gives the orders.
COW	This is our farm- not Napoleon's.
NARRATOR 1	The farm was filled with fear and rumors.
PIGEON	I've seen Snowball!
HEN	Squealer says he steals corn and milk. He broke eggs and is eating the fruit from the trees.
BENJAMIN (DONKEY)	Do you still believe anything Squealer says?

COW I've heard that Snowball creeps into our stalls and milks us in our sleep.

MURIEL (GOAT) That's stupid.

NARRATOR 3 It was Snowball's fault whenever anything went wrong,

SQUEALER (PIG) Comrades, Snowball has been with Jones all the time! Snowball is plotting with the humans to attack us and take the farm back!

CLOVER (HORSE) But Snowball was a hero! He led the charge at the Battle of the Cowshed...

SQUEALER (PIG) Comrades, Comrades, Comrades, it is written down in secret documents.

BENJAMIN (DONKEY) What documents? Where are these documents?

SQUEALER (PIG) If you could read – I would show you the documents.

CLOVER (HORSE) ...and he was wounded. We all saw the blood.

SQUEALER (PIG)   Jones only grazed him. Can't you see? That was part of the plot with Jones. Comrade Napoleon was the real hero that day.

MURIEL (GOAT)   Snowball is no traitor. He was a good comrade.

NARRATOR 1   Napoleon emerged from the farmhouse, wearing his medals, his snarling guard dogs followed.

PINCHER (DOG)   Look! He's even wearing the medals of the sheep that died in the Battle of the Cowshed.

NARRATOR 2   He ordered all animals to assemble in the yard.

JESSIE (DOG)   The Geese are with Napoleon?

NARRATOR 3   All geese were dragged out in terror because all the geese had protested when Napoleon abolished meetings.

BENJAMIN (DONKEY)   What's Napoleon going to do?

MURIEL (GOAT)   You know what he's going to do.

NARRATOR 1   The geese waited, trembling.

NAPOLEON (PIG)   CONFESS YOUR CRIMES.

GEESE   We have been secretly plotting with Snowball, we helped him destroy the windmill. We agreed to hand over Animal Farm to Snowball and Jones.

NAPOLEON (PIG)   ...AND?

GEESE   ...and Snowball has been with Jones from the beginning.

NARRATOR 2   Napoleon's eyes darted toward the dogs, and the dogs jumped onto the geese and tore all their throats out.

COW	This can't be happening!
BENJAMIN (DONKEY)	It's happening.
HEN	We are next, I think.
NARRATOR 3	Those hens who had been leaders in the rebellion of the eggs were dragged forward.
NAPOLEON (PIG)	CONFESS!
HENS	We stole corn from the harvest and ate it all at night...
NARRATOR 1	They, too, were then slaughtered. More hens- more geese were dragged forward. The confessions and executions went on,
BENJAMIN (DONKEY)	No animal shall kill another.
NARRATOR 3	The air was filled with the smell of blood; a smell unknown since Joneses time.

BLUEBELL (DOG)　　　I can't believe this is happening on our farm. It must be us. Some fault in us. From now on I will get up a full hour earlier in the mornings and work harder.

CLOVER (HORSE)　　　This was not what Old Major wanted.

BENJAMIN (DONKEY)　　　Your dream, not mine. Free from hunger and free from the whip, all equal...I never believed it.

SQUEALER (PIG)　　　But comrades, this is paradise! The society we all dreamed about is here. THIS IS SUGARCANDY MOUNTAIN!

SHEEP　　　Four legs good, two legs bad.

SQUEALER (PIG)　　　From now on, the gun will be fired every year on Napoleon's birthday.

NARRATOR 1 On Sunday mornings Squealer, holding down a long strip of paper with one of his trotters, would read out statistics proving that production of food had increased by two hundred percent, three hundred percent, five hundred percent.

CLOVER (HORSE) We need fewer numbers and more food.

JESSIE (DOG) We work longer now and the food is no better than when Jones was here.

MURIEL (GOAT) They say Napoleon has two of his dogs serving him and eats from Mrs. Jones' China plates.

COW I heard a young pig named Pinkeye tastes all his food first, in case it's been poisoned.

SQUEALER (PIG) Hail comrade Napoleon, the Father and Protector of All Animals.

NARRATOR 2 Squealer would talk with tears rolling down his fat cheeks about Napoleon's goodness - his deep love for all animals, and giving Napoleon the credit for every small achievement.

SQUEALER (PIG) How excellent water tastes these days, thanks to the leadership of Comrade Napoleon.

NARRATOR 3 By autumn, the windmill was finished, now named Napoleon Mill.

BENJAMIN (DONKEY) Napoleon Mill, I am glad Boxer's not here to see.

NARRATOR 1 The long-expected second human attack finally came. Bravely the animals marched, but there were fifteen men, with guns, and the animals were soon driven back.

JESSIE(DOG) Our windmill is in the hands of the enemy.

MURIEL (GOAT)　　Two humans have brought hammers. They're going to break down the windmill.

NAPOLEON (PIG)　　Impossible! I...we... have built the walls thicker this time. Have courage comrades!

BENJAMIN (DONKEY)　　They are not trying to knock it down. They are making holes for explosives.

NARRATOR 3　　There was a deafening roar.

BLUEBELL (DOG)　　What was that?

JESSIE(DOG)　　Pigeons, go look.

NARRATOR 2　　The pigeons swirled into the air.

NARRATOR 1　　There was another deafening roar All animals, except Napoleon, flung themselves on the ground and hid their faces.

CLOVER (HORSE)　　Look at Napoleon, he's not afraid.

BLUEBELL (DOG)　　Maybe he knows something we don't?

NARRATOR 3 The animals' courage soon returned. Fear was replaced with rage. A cow, three sheep, and two pigeons had been killed and everyone was wounded.

NARRATOR 2 Three men had their heads broken by Clover's hoofs; another speared by a cow's horn; another his trousers ripped off by Jessie and Bluebell.

NARRATOR 3 At that moment, Napoleon's dog bodyguard jumped on the men, snarling and biting. The men ran for their lives,

BLUEBELL (DOG) Look they are running away.

JESSIE(DOG) Did you see me? Did you see me? I've still got some of his trousers in my teeth.

PINCHER (DOG) WE WON!

BENJAMIN (DONKEY) Call this winning? Look around.

NARRATOR 1	The animals looked around. The sight of dead comrades moved all to tears.
NARRATOR 2	Then there was the booming of a gun behind them in the farmyard.
BENJAMIN (DONKEY)	Why is that gun firing?
SQUEALER (PIG)	To celebrate the victory, comrades!
BENJAMIN (DONKEY)	What victory?
SQUEALER	Comrades, have we not driven the enemy off our sacred Animal Farm?
BLUEBELL (DOG)	They have destroyed the windmill.
CLOVER (HORSE)	Did anyone see the humans destroy the windmill?
BENJAMIN (DONKEY)	Maybe we should find out?

SQUEALER (PIG)   Thanks to the leadership of Comrade Napoleon we can build six windmills. We have won our farm back again!

MURIEL (GOAT)   We only won back what we had before.

SQUEALER (PIG)   It will be called the Battle of the Windmill, and our leader, Napoleon, will create a new medal, the Order of the Green Banner,

BENJAMIN (DONKEY)   Which he will give to himself.

NARRATOR 1   The pigs were dancing and singing in the yard after buying another case of whisky.

COW   Come and see this!

NARRATOR 2   The animals looked down on the yard from their work in the field.

CLOVER (HORSE)   I don't want to look.

NARRATOR 3 All but clover stopped work and looked at the drunken pigs with shame.

BENJAMIN (DONKEY) Nothing's changed.

BLUEBELL (DOG) We're all still hungry

MURIEL (GOAT) We still sleep on straw.

PINCHER (DOG) We still work in the field.

JESSIE(DOG) In winter we're still cold

COW In summer, still troubled by flies.

NARRATOR 1 They remembered the old days, the expulsion of Jones, the Seven Commandments, and great battles with the humans. None of the old dreams had been forgotten.

CLOVER (HORSE) Yes, we work harder now, but at least we can work for ourselves.

JESSIE(DOG) We are all equal.

NARRATOR 2	It was a pleasant evening as the animals walked back to the farm.

Suddenly, they saw all the pigeons flying overhead and swooping.

PIGEON	COME QUICK! YOU WON'T BELIEVE IT!

NARRATOR 3	All the animals galloped down from the field into the yard. Then they saw it for themselves.

CLOVER (HORSE)	LOOK! THAT PIG IS WALKING UPRIGHT ON HIS BACK LEGS.

BENJAMIN (DONKEY)	Is that Squealer?

JESSIE(DOG)	Look! More pigs are coming out of the house trying to walk on their back legs,

BENJAMIN (DONKEY)	Is that Napoleon?

MURIEL (GOAT)	What is he wearing?

JESSIE(DOG)	He's wearing Jones' old suit. The one he wore for weddings and funerals.

CLOVER (HORSE)   Look! He's carrying a whip in his trotter.

NARRATOR 1   The animals looked on in horror as Humans came out of the house too, carrying bottles. All were drunk. The animals angrily chanted.

CLOVER (HORSE)   WHATEVER GOES UPON FOUR LEGS…OR HAS WINGS…IS A FRIEND.

BENJAMIN (DONKEY)   NO ANIMAL SHALL WEAR CLOTHES.

BLUEBELL (DOG)   NO ANIMAL SHALL SLEEP IN A BED.

JESSIE(DOG)   NO ANIMAL SHALL DRINK ALCOHOL.

PINCHER (DOG)   NO ANIMAL SHALL KILL ANY OTHER ANIMAL.

MURIEL (GOAT)   ALL ANIMALS ARE EQUAL.

SHEEP   FOUR LEGS GOOD, TWO LEGS BETTER! FOUR LEGS GOOD, TWO LEGS BETTER!

NARRATOR 3   Benjamin felt a nose nuzzling at his shoulder. He looked round. It was Clover. Her old eyes looked dimmer than ever. She tugged gently at his mane and led him round to the end of the big barn, where the Seven Commandments were written.

CLOVER (HORSE)   My sight is failing. Even when I was young, I couldn't read what was written. But it seems to me that that wall looks different. Are the Seven Commandments the same as they used to be, Benjamin?

NARRATOR 1   For once Benjamin consented to break his rule, and he read out to her what was written on the wall. There was nothing there now except one single Commandment.

BENJAMIN (HORSE)

ALL ANIMALS ARE EQUAL, BUT SOME ANIMALS ARE MORE EQUAL THAN OTHERS.

ACT ONE
STUDY QUESTIONS (KS3)
CAMBRIDGE EXAMINATIONS

1. **In Act One (page 10),** Old Major says "Comrades, I shall not be with you much longer." Who is Old Major talking to when he uses the word -comrades?

    a) All animals and humans.
    b) The pigs
    c) All animals

2. In Act One (page 14), Old Major says "Man serves the interests of no creature but himself." What does this mean?

    a) Man thinks he is interesting.
    b) Humans just look after themselves.
    c) Men are selfish.

3. **In Act One (pages 26 -27),** Which of the following Commandments was **NOT** written on the barn door?

    a) NO HUMAN SHALL KILL ANY ANIMAL
    b) NO ANIMAL SHALL KILL ANY OTHER ANIMAL.
    c) NO ANIMAL SHALL DRINK ALCOHOL.
    d) NO ANIMAL SHALL SLEEP IN A BED.
    e) NO ANIMAL SHALL WEAR CLOTHES.

4. **TEXT SEARCH: Act One (page 28), Fill in the missing verbs.**

All cheered. Horses _____, sheep and goats bleated, the raven _____, donkeys _____, dogs barked, geese _____, pigs grunted, hens clucked, and pigeons _____.

Read this short biography and answer the questions.

Eric Arthur Blair was born on 25th June 1903, in British-occupied India. At school, he was an average student. After an unhappy time at Eton, he left without a diploma.

The Blair family encouraged their son to apply for the Indian Imperial Police because of his limited prospects. After further studies, he was able to pass the entrance examination and start work for the Imperial Police in 1922.

Orwell started writing 'Animal Farm' in the 1940s, during the second world war, when Russia was an ally of the British and Americans in their war against Hitler. It was after the war, in 1949, that he finally published 'Animal Farm'.

5. **What qualifications did Eric Blair have when he left school?**

    a) Diploma
    b) None
    c) Certificate

6. **What was Eric Blair's first job?**

    a) Army
    b) Writer
    c) Police

7. **What year was Animal Farm published?**

    a) 1949
    b) 1940
    c) 1922

8. **Use a quote from Act One (page 17),** The Narrator tells us that Old Major had died. Where was Old Major buried?

_____

9. **Use a quote from Act One (page 18),** What was the 'badge' of Mollie's slavery?

_____

10. **Use a quote from Act One (page 26),** Napoleon orders that the Farm should be called Animal Farm. What was the farm's name before?

_____

TEACHER ASSESSED WRITING RESPONSE

"… the pigeons had been ordered to fly to all the neighboring farms with the story of the rebellion."

Instructions: instead of pigeons, you have been asked to send a message telling all the animals on neighboring farms about what happened on Animal Farm. Your message should be no more than 20-25 words. You can also mention what the animals hope for in the future.

To: All Animals

From:

Subject:

_____

_____

_____

_____

_____

_____

_____

ACT TWO

STUDY QUESTIONS (KS3)
CAMBRIDGE EXAMINATIONS

Key Vocabulary:

Authoritarian- [or-thor-a-tarian] Strict obedience to one leader.

Communism – [com-mune-izm] All property is owned by the people and each person works and is paid according to their abilities and needs.

Corruption – [korr-up-shon] Dishonest behavior especially by powerful people.

Propaganda – [as written] The spreading of biased, misleading, or false ideas.

Rebellion- [as written] The action of resisting authority.

Symbolism – [sim-boll-izm]   The idea that things represent other things.

1, Napoleon's leadership style can be described as:

    a) Authoritarian
    b) Communism
    c) Rebellion

2. When Squealer wants to control the animals with speech, he uses:

    a) Symbolism
    b) Corruption
    c) Propaganda

3. When the animals force Jones off the farm this is called:

   a) Authoritarian
   b) Rebellion
   c) Corruption

In Act Two (page 37), "Snowball, calm in the swirls of churning dust kicked up by panicking hooves, had been expecting this. He'd studied an old book on Julius Caesar which he'd found in the farmhouse. He gave his orders."

4. Why did Snowball read a book about Julius Caesar?

   a) To learn about ancient Rome.
   b) To learn how to rule an empire.
   c) To learn how to make war.

5. In Act Two (page 39), Snowball tells Boxer. "…war is war". What does Snowball most likely mean?

   a) In war, you have to be cruel.
   b) Things happen in war that can't always be controlled.
   c) You have to do anything to win.

Mollie's Diary

On the day Mollie left the farm, she wrote in her diary but her grammar is bad. Can you help Mollie to correct her grammar mistakes?

*"I am so unhappy. I miss Mr. Jones. He **[6] give** me sugar and nice ribbons to wear in my mane. On **[7] Sunday's**, he took me **[8] in** the village and all the children would give me sugar.*

6)

    a) gave
    b) given
    c) gives

7)

    a) Sunday
    b) Sundays'
    c) Sundays

8)

    a) for
    b) to
    c) at

9) TEXT SEARCH: in Act Two (page 40), when Napoleon was giving medals, who was awarded "…Animal Hero, Second Class…"?

    a) Snowball
    b) Boxer
    c) Sheep

10) TEXT SEARCH: in Act Two (page 43), who first had the idea to build a windmill?

    a) Napoleon
    b) Snowball
    c) Squealer

In Act Two (page 48), "At the same moment, a terrible howling, as nine enormous dogs wearing brass-studded collars came bounding into the barn.

11) Where did the dogs come from?

- a) They were stray puppies from the village.
- b) Napoleon found the puppies and brought them up to be his guard dogs.
- c) They were the puppies of Jessie and Bluebell.

ACT THREE
STUDY QUESTIONS (KS3)
CAMBRIDGE EXAMINATION

In Act Three (page 53), BOXER (HORSE) "If Comrade Napoleon says it is right, it must be right. Napoleon is always right; I will work harder. We must all work harder."

1 Why does Boxer want to believe Napoleon?

    a) He wants the farm to be a success.

    b) He has known Napoleon for a long time.

    c) Boxer is not very clever.

In Act Three (page 57), SQUEALER (PIG) Comrades, we pigs should have a quiet place to work. It is better for Napoleon, our leader, to be seen, by the humans, living in a house, not a dirty old shed.

BENJAMIN (DONKEY) **The dirty old shed is good enough for us, though.**

2 What does Benjamin mean?

    a) He means he is happy living in the shed and that all animals should be happy living in a shed.
    b) If the shed is dirty and old, why do all the other animals have to live in it?
    c) He wants the shed to be improved, so all animals will be comfortable living there.

In Act Three (pages 58-59), MURIEL (GOAT) It says, 'No animal shall sleep in a bed *with sheets*.' Muriel has noticed that the original commandment has been changed.

3 What was the original commandment?

    a) No animal shall sleep in a bed.
    b) No one shall sleep in a bed with sheets.
    c) No animal shall sleep in a bed without sheets.

TEXT SEARCH: In Act Two (page 59), Muriel has noticed that other commandments have also been changed. Write these changes to the original commandments.

Original: "No animal shall drink alcohol."

4_____

Original: "No animal shall kill any other animal"

5 _____

Reading

Squealer, a clever pig, speaks for Napoleon. He serves as Napoleon's Minister of Propaganda. Every time orders from Napoleon are questioned by the other animals —Squealer can convince the animals that Napoleon is only acting in their best interests. For example, after Squealer is questioned about Napoleon's stealing the milk and apples, he explains that many pigs " dislike milk and apples" and tells the animals, "It is for your sake that we drink that milk and eat those apples."

6 Which statement is the most accurate?

a) Squealer's job is to lie.
b) Squealer's job is to twist the truth.
c) Squealer's job is to keep the animals away from Napoleon.

7 Squealer tries to convince the animals that "It is for your sake that we drink that milk and eat those apples." What is he trying to make the animals believe?

a) The pigs are making a sacrifice for the good of the animals.
b) The pigs are saving the animals from harmful milk and apples.
c) Pigs need apples and milk more than other animals.

ACT FOUR

STUDY QUESTIONS

iGCSE EXAMINATION

1. **TEXT SEARCH: Act 4: Page 67.** What evidence is there in the text, on this page, for the friendship between Boxer and Benjamin? Use quotes from the text.

　_____

　_____

　_____

　_____

　_____

2. **TEXT SEARCH: Act 4: Page 68.** Moses describes Sugarcandy Mountain. What is Boxer's reaction? Use quotes from the text.

　_____

　_____

　_____

　_____

　_____

3. **TEXT SEARCH: Act 4: Page 71.** How does Squealer use Boxer's death as propaganda? Use Squealer's own words to support your opinion.

ACT FIVE

STUDY QUESTIONS

iGCSE EXAMINATION

TEACHER ASSESSED WRITING RESPONSE

Act 5: pages 75-76. In your own words, what do you think the animal's opinion is of Minimus' poem?

_____

_____

_____

1. Act 5: pages 77- 78. There are rumors about Snowball. Which of the following rumors is not mentioned in the text on those pages?

    a) eats the fruit from the trees
    b) steals corn and milk
    c) sends secret documents
    d) milks the cows at night

Act 5: pages 90-91.   JESSIE(DOG) "Look! More pigs are coming out of the house trying to walk on their back legs,

    BENJAMIN (DONKEY) "Is that Napoleon?"

    CLOVER (HORSE) "Look! He's carrying a whip in his trotter."

TEACHER ASSESSED WRITING RESPONSE

It is symbolically significant that Napoleon is trying to walk on his hind legs, wearing Jones' wedding suit, and carrying a whip. In your own words, what is Orwell trying to say with this image of Napoleon?

TEACHER ASSESSED WRITING RESPONSE

ALL ANIMALS ARE EQUAL, BUT SOME ANIMALS ARE MORE EQUAL THAN OTHERS.

In your own words, explain what this means.

_____

_____

_____

_____

_____

_____

_____

_____

_____

_____

_____

_____

_____

_____

IELTS READING STUDY QUESTIONS

Vocabulary

dystopian *- imagined society with great suffering or injustice*

allegory *–one thing represents another, animals representing humans.*

Totalitarianism *- citizens totally subject to an authority*

Subservience *- believing that your own needs are less important than those of others.*

Reading

[A] Animal Farm is a dystopian allegory based on events that occurred during the Russian revolution of 1917. In this sense, all the events that occur within the novel, such as the farm animals rebelling against their farm owner Mr. Jones, can be seen as an extended metaphor for the events of 1917.

[B] Orwell assigns the central character traits that represent key players within the Soviet Communism party. For example, Napoleon represents Joseph Stalin becoming leader of the farm, In Orwell's novel, Napoleon can be seen to take a totalitarianism approach, where he dictates to the other animals exactly what is expected and expects complete subservience in return.

[C} Despite a short-lived period of "utopia", Orwell ends the novel in a very similar way to how it began, with the animals suffering at the hands of their leaders. This is a clear critique from Orwell of the Russian Revolution as the change in leadership has done very little to improve the lifestyle of the citizens but has only benefited its leaders.

TRUE if the statement is true according to the passage

FALSE, if the statement contradicts the passage

NOT GIVEN if there is no information about this

1. In paragraph [A], the events in Animal farm are compared to the events in the Russian Revolution.
   a) True
   b) False
   c) Not Given

2. In paragraph [B], like Stalin in Russia, Napoleon becomes the leader of Animal Farm
   a) True
   b) False
   c) Not Given

3. In paragraph [C], Orwell ends his novel with a warning for the future.
   a) True
   b) False
   c) Not Given

4. In paragraph [A}, what is described as 'dystopian'?
   a) Russia
   b) Animal Farm
   c) Mr. Jones

5. In paragraph [B}, the word-*subservience*-can be replaced with:

a) expects complete admiration in return.
b) expects complete respect in return.
c) expects complete obedience in return.

6. In paragraph [C], whom did Orwell think benefited most from the Russian Revolution?

a) The people
b) The leaders
c) The citizens

Complete each of the following sentences with information from the 'Reading' passage. Write No MORE THAN ONE OR TWO words for each answer.

Animal Farm is a fable with a message, and represents the people and events from the **[7]** _____.

Orwell gives each animal the character **[8]** _____ of people within the Soviet Communism party.

This **[9]** _____ didn't last, Orwell ends the novel with pessimism.

ACT ONE
IELTS STUDY QUESTIONS

Act One: IELTS study questions

In Act One (page 9), The narrator informs us about "Those animals wanting to avoid the intoxicated attentions of Jones, quietly crept into the barn, making themselves as comfortable as fur, feathers, hooves, and horns would allow."

1. **What does the narrator probably mean by "avoid the intoxicated attentions"?**
a) When Jones was drunk, he shouted at the animals.
b) When Jones was drunk, the animals felt uncomfortable
c) When Jones was drunk, he did not treat the animals well.

In Act One (page 9), Old Major is described as, "the majestic old hog... highly regarded by the animals, and there was a respectful silence as they waited for Old Major to speak."

2. **In this context, why was silence a sign of respect?**
a) The animals agree with Old Major and support him.
b) The animals attach great importance to Old Major's words.
c) Old Major is their leader and should be respected.

In Act One (page 11), Old Major, in his speech to the animals he claims, "Here, no animal is free. Jones destroys families, consumes without producing, withholds food, kills the weak, and prevents us from even owning our own bodies with humiliating rings in our noses, harnesses, bits, spurs, and the whip.

3. **What does Old Major refer to when he says, "...prevents us from even owning our own bodies..."?**
   a) Making the animals wear humiliating objects like harnesses and ribbons makes them slaves.
   b) Jones saw the animals as nothing but profit.
   c) To Jones, the animals are no more than property.

4. **In Act One (page 11), why does the author, through the narrator, describe Mollie as, '...the foolish, pretty white mare was chewing a lump of sugar. She had placed herself near the front and began flicking her white mane from side to side, hoping to draw attention to the red ribbons she was wearing.**

   a) The character of Mollie represents the Russian Royal family.
   b) The character of Mollie represents the middle classes that did not support the Russian Revolution and left Russia.
   c) The character of Mollie represents all those who do not see any need for change.

5. **In Act One (page 13), Old Major uses rhetorical techniques. Which rhetorical technique is Old Major using here, "…Is it because we are stupid? Is it because humans are superior? Is it because this farm is poor?" (you may need a dictionary)**

    a) caricature
    b) hyperbole
    c) The rule of three

In Act One (page 18), Snowball, Napoleon, and Squealer turned old Major's words into a new philosophy. They called this new way of thinking 'Animalism'.

6. **For Orwell, 'Animalism' represents:**
    a) Fascism
    b) Communism
    c) Liberalism

"… Some animals loved to hear his comforting stories about animal heaven - Sugarcandy Mountain."

7. What is the most likely reason that some animals 'loved' the stories about 'Sugar Candy Mountain"?

    a) Because they were religious.
    b) Because they liked stories
    c) Because the stories were about hope.

8. **Which character, in Act One said,**" ... Mollie, the horse, won't learn more than the six letters in her own name..." (Page 31)
    a) Napoleon
    b) Squealer
    c) Narrator

9. **Which character in Act One said,** "...We drink milk and eat apples for you. It is our sacrifice for you..." (Page 33)
    a) Napoleon
    b) Squealer
    c) Narrator

ACT TWO
IELTS STUDY QUESTIONS

Act Two: IELTS Study Questions

1 In Act Two (page 36), the local farmers...had no interest in Jones' drunken self-pity but were interested in his failing farm …" **Why were the local farmers interested in Jones' farm?**

   a) The farmers want to buy the farm
   b) The farmers want to sell the farm
   c) The farmers want to run the farm

TEXT SEARCH: in Act Two (page 36), Jones makes some predictions about what will happen on the farm if he is not there.

2 What prediction, by Jones, is NOT mentioned in the play?

   a) Torture
   b) Murder
   c) Starvation
   d) cannibalism

In Act Two (page 36), The sheep repeat a propaganda slogan, **"Four legs good, two legs bad."**

3 Remembering the context, which of the following is the best explanation of what the slogan means?

   a) Creatures that have four legs have a physical advantage over those with two legs.
   b) Creatures that have two legs are inferior.
   c) Humans are the enemy.

4 TEXT SEARCH: In Act Two (page 45), at first, Napoleon does not like the idea of the animals building a windmill because:

   a) he does not want them too tired to work.
   b) he needs them to farm for food.
   c) he needs them working so they can't get ideas.

5 TEXT SEARCH: In Act Two (page 49). Why does Napoleon ban meetings in the yard?

   a) He wants the animals to salute the flag.
   b) He doesn't like animals talking and getting ideas
   c) He wants the animals to work not talk.

IELTS Listening: Part 4. You will listen to a university lecturer giving a talk to her students on, 'The Inevitability of Totalitarianism in Animal Farm. Listen to the lecture and answer the questions.

Good morning. Today I want to talk to you about George Orwell's pessimistic belief that totalitarianism was inevitable. According to Russell Baker, who wrote the preface to Animal Farm's 1996, Orwell's pessimism stemmed from his having grown up in an age of dictatorship. Orwell witnessed Hitler's and Stalin's movements from afar, as well as fighting totalitarianism himself in the Spanish Civil War, Orwell came to believe in the rise of a new species of autocrat, worse even than the tyrants of old. His cynicism is reflected in both his novels, 'Animal Farm' and '1984'.

Orwell emphasizes the insidiousness of totalitarianism early in the novel when the pigs take the fresh milk and apples.

The pigs justify their actions on the basis of their superiority; they are smart and need more nutrition than the other animals to fuel their brainpower. Orwell makes the point that totalitarianism need not be blatant in order to be operating. It can hide under the guise of the "greater good" as it did in the Soviet Union before the totalitarianism became obvious. The novel begins with Jones as an autocratic tyrant and ends with Napoleon not only in Jones's position but in his clothes as well.

6 What two ideas does the lecturer offer as reasons for Orwell's pessimism?

   a) Living at the same time as Hitler and Stalin, and fighting in a civil war.

   b) Believing there was a new species of tyrant and studying Communism.

   c) Growing up in the 1930s and hating war.

7 What book listed here was NOT mentioned in the lecture?

   a) A New Species of Autocrat

   b) 1984

   c) Animal Farm

8 How does the lecturer use the phrase "greater good" (Dictionary)

   a) comically

   b) ironically

   c) Angrily

ACT THREE
TOEFL STUDY QUESTIONS

Vocabulary

Infer- the most logical conclusion from the information given.

Imply- clues in the information lead you to believe that…

In Act Three (Page 52) Squealer says, "Comrades! Loyalty and obedience are more important. One false step and our enemies will be upon us! Surely, comrades, you don't want Jones back!"

1. Squealer implies that:

a) Loyalty and obedience are good qualities.
b) disobedience has negative consequences.
c) Jones is the only enemy.

In Act Three (pages 58-59) Muriel wants to know who and why there have been changes to the commandments. "No animal shall drink alcohol." Now it reads, "No animal shall drink too much alcohol." "No animal shall kill any other animal" They've changed that to, "No animal shall kill any other animal without cause."

2. It can be reasonably inferred?

a) The pigs changed the commandments because they wanted to drink alcohol and harm the other animals.
b) The pigs changed the commandments because they wanted to correct earlier mistakes in the writing.
c) They changed the commandments to make them more human-like.

In Act Three (page 62) Boxer defends the pigs. "They work hard in their own way. They are clever. They organize everything. Napoleon is always right.

3. Boxer infers that:

a) Napoleon and the pigs are never wrong.
b) Being clever and organized is the pig's job.
c) Boxer is happy with Napoleon's leadership.

In Act Three (page 62) the play gives us evidence that the narrator is not unbiased and has opinions. "The animals got thinner and weaker, except Napoleon and the pigs who got fatter and stronger. Instead of food, there were more songs, more speeches, more processions, and worse of all more poetry."

4. Identify the narrator's biased opinion.

a) "… except Napoleon and the pigs…"
b) "…more songs, more speeches, more processions…"
c) "…and worse of all more poetry."

5 The Sheep's latest slogan in Act Three is, "Long live Comrade Napoleon!" Is it significant that "Long live Animal Farm" is now "Long live Comrade Napoleon!"?

a) Yes, it means that the sheep are very loyal to Napoleon.

b) No, because the sheep's chanting is meaningless.

c) Yes, because the change is from long live the whole community to long live one individual.

ACT FOUR

TOEFL STUDY QUESTIONS

In Act Four (page 66), SQUEALER (PIG) Two dozen apples to any animal who captures him alive!

MURIEL (GOAT) I thought there were no apples left.

1. What is Muriel implying?

    a) that the animals will not help to capture Snowball.
    b) that Squealer lied about the apples
    c) that Squealer will have to change the reward.

TEACHER ASSESSED WRITING RESPONSE

In Act Four (page 68), Moses describes Sugarcandy Mountain to Boxer after he has fallen sick.

"Up there, Boxer, just on the other side of the clouds is Sugarcandy Mountain, that happy country where we poor animals shall rest forever. I have seen it. I flew so high once I saw it myself. Everlasting fields of grass. Cake and sugar growing on trees."

Orwell himself rejected all religious belief as a sign of "intellectual immaturity". In Animal Farm, Orwell uses Sugarcandy Mountain to represent religion.

Is Sugarcandy Mountain a negative or positive view of the role of religion in society? Discuss the question in your own words and with your own opinions.

In Act Four (page 70), Squealer claims that he was with Boxer when he died. "I was at his bedside. He whispered in my ear. "Forward, comrades. Long live Animal Farm! Long live Comrade Napoleon! Napoleon is always right." Those were his very last words, comrades."

2 This is most likely an example of:

   a) Propaganda
   b) Exaggeration
   c) Lying

In Act Four (page 71), Muriel is angry. "There was never going to be a peaceful retirement up on the pasture for Boxer…quiet evenings learning the alphabet. THERE WAS NO HOSPITAL! THEY SOLD BOXER TO THE BUTCHER, FOR WHISKEY."

TEACHER ASSESSED WRITING RESPONSE

Do you agree or disagree with either or both of these opinions about Boxer?

   i. Boxer was a tragic idealist who believed in the promise of the revolution, worked himself nearly to death for it, and was used and betrayed by an uncaring tyrant.
   ii. Boxer died because of his own ignorance. It was his hope for the best attitude that got him killed in the end.

ACT FIVE

TOEFL STUDY QUESTIONS

In Act 5: (Page 83) The Narrator tells us, "On Sunday mornings Squealer, holding down a long strip of paper with one of his trotters, would read out statistics proving that production of food had increased by two hundred percent, three hundred percent, five hundred percent."

1. **How is Orwell using statistics?**

   a) To support the idea that Squealer always tries to turn bad news into a propaganda tool.

   b) To lie about how much is being produced to justify selling food outside.

In Act 5: (Page 84) the Narrator describes how Squealer would talk. "… with tears rolling down his fat cheeks about Napoleon's goodness - his deep love for all animals, and giving Napoleon the credit for every small achievement.

2. The phrase " …and **giving Napoleon the credit** for every small achievement." is closest in meaning to…

   a) "…and Napoleon is responsible for everything on the farm."
   b) "…and giving Napoleon the benefit from every small achievement. "
   c) "…and we should thank Napoleon for every achievement."

3. In Act 5: (Page 91) What is the significance of the new slogan chanted by the sheep to the plot development in Animal Farm?

"FOUR LEGS GOOD, TWO LEGS BETTER! FOUR LEGS GOOD, TWO LEGS BETTER!"

a) The change reflects the gradual move away from the principles of Animalism.
b) The sheep represent ignorance.
c) The sheep are reflecting the changing character of the pigs and their embrace of human values.

ACT ONE

SAT QUESTIONS

ACT 1: Brief Synopsis

Mr. Jones is the owner of Manor Farm. All the farm animals meet in the big barn to hear a speech by Old Major, Old Major blames the [1] animals' suffering on humans. Mr. Jones, thinking that a fox is in the yard, fires a shot [2] (using a shotgun) into the side of the barn. The animals go to sleep, and the Manor Farm again is quiet.

Old Major [3] dies in his sleep. The animals make secret preparations to take the farm from Mr. Jones. Napoleon, Snowball, and Squealer create the principles of Animalism. The animals call one another "Comrade". One day, Mr. Jones goes on a drinking binge and forgets to feed the animals. Unable to bear their hunger, the cows complain about conditions. Mr. Jones discovers this and begins to whip the animals. Spurred into anger, the animals turn on him and easily chase him from the farm. The animals hurry to destroy the last remaining evidence of their subservience: They explore the empty farmhouse, in stunned silence at the unbelievable luxuries within. From then on, "Manor Farm" will be known as "Animal Farm." [4] Meanwhile, Snowball and Napoleon, reduce the principles of Animalism to seven key commandments. The animals go to gather the harvest, but the cows haven't been milked. When the animals return that evening, the milk has disappeared.

1)

    a) NO CHANGE

    b) animal's

    c) animals

    d) animal

2)

    a) NO CHANGE

    b) (using a shotgun):

    c) (using a shotgun),

    d) (using a shotgun).

3)

Which choice most effectively combines the sentences at the underlined portion?

    a) dies in his sleep, and the animals

    b) dies in his sleep; the animals

    c) dies in his sleep -the animals

    d) dies in his sleep: the animals

4)

    a) NO CHANGE

    b) For example,

    c) Furthermore,

    d) At any rate,

ACT TWO
SAT QUESTIONS

ACT 2: Brief Synopsis

The animals spend summer harvesting in the fields. Boxer does most of the heavy labor, adopting "I will work harder!" as a personal motto. **[1]** <u>Of all</u> the animals, only Benjamin, the obstinate donkey, seems to recognize no change under the new leadership. Every Sunday, the animals hold a flag-raising ceremony. The flag's green background represents fields, and its white hoof and horn symbolize the animals. Snowball **[2]** <u>starts to establish</u> several committees and educational classes. The classes designed to teach to read and write meet with some success. Boxer never gets beyond the letter D. When it becomes apparent that many of the animals are unable to memorize the Seven Commandments, Snowball reduces the principles to one essential maxim: "Four legs good, two legs bad." <u>The Clean Tails League for the cows, and the Wild Comrades Re-education Committee are the least attended</u>. **[3]**

The animals discover that the pigs have been taking all of the milk and apples for themselves. Squealer explains that pigs need milk and apples to think well, The pigeons alerted Animal Farm that Mr. Jones **[4]** <u>has begun</u> marching on the farm with some men. Snowball, who has studied books about the battle campaigns of the Roman general Julius Caesar, prepares a defense. Snowball wants to build a windmill, bringing new comforts to the animals. Napoleon has other plans and invites Snowball to the barn. attack Snowball, and chase him off the farm. Napoleon announces that meetings will be held only for ceremonial purposes. He states that all important decisions will be his.

1)
   a) NO CHANGE
   b) In all
   c) All of
   d) So

2)
   a) NO CHANGE
   b) establishes
   c) starts established
   d) starts to establishing

3)

The writer wants to add a concluding sentence that restates the main idea of the passage. Which choice best accomplishes this goal?

   a) NO CHANGE
   b) The literacy classes, teaching reading, and writing were the most popular
   c) Animalism, will prove to be a philosophy that evolves.
   d) All the animals looked forward to sharing the rewards of their first harvest together.

4)

    a) NO CHANGE

    b) had begun,

    c) is beginning,

    d) will begin,

In Act Two (page 41), The narrator talks about Mollie. "As winter drew on, Mollie became more and more troublesome. She was late for work every morning and excused herself by saying that she had overslept, or complained of mysterious pains, although her appetite was, obviously, excellent.

5 What is implied in this extract?

    a) Mollie is unfit to work on Animal Farm.

    b) Mollie misses her old life under Mr. Jones.

    c) Mollie is increasingly opposed to Animal Farm.

6 In Act Two (page 45), Napoleon confides to Squealer "If the windmill is successful, and the animals have their workload decreased, they will be able to relax."

The only thing that can be reasonably inferred is that:

- a) The animal's relaxation may not be a positive development for Napoleon.
- b) Napoleon would like the animals to work harder.
- c) that the windmill may have a direct result on the length of the animal's working day.

In Act Two (page 48), Napoleon addresses the animals in the yard. "These meetings you like to have in the yard will have to end. Talking together like that. All animals will gather every week to salute the flag, but no more ideas. No more talking. Leave the thinking to us."

7 It can be reasonably inferred that:

- a) Napoleon does not want the animals to think for themselves.
- b) Napoleon believes he should make all the decisions.
- c) Napoleon does not like the animals talking during the flag ceremony.

ACT THREE

SAT QUESTIONS

Act 3: Brief Synopsis

The animals learn that Napoleon supports the windmill project. **[1]** <u>Squealer clarifies and explains that their</u> leader never really opposed the proposal; he simply used his opposition as a maneuver to oust the wicked Snowball.

The farm still needs many items that it cannot produce on its own. Napoleon announces that he has hired a human solicitor, Mr. Whimper, to assist in conducting trade. The pigs begin living in the farmhouse and sleep in beds. Clover asks Muriel to read the commandment and finds that it now reads "No animal shall sleep in a bed with sheets. The windmill has been destroyed. Napoleon blames Snowball and passes a death sentence on Snowball. Napoleon contracts to sell four hundred eggs a week. The **[2]** <u>affect</u> of this demand is that the hens' rebel. Napoleon stages a purge: forcing certain animals to confess to a conspiracy with Snowball and are killed by the dogs.

Boxer says that the tragedy must owe to some fault **[3}** <u>in the animals themselves; he commits to working even harder</u>. The commandment reading "No animal shall kill any other animal" now reads: "No animal shall kill any other animal without cause." The humans attack the farm again. Enraged, the animals attack the men, driving them away, but several animals are killed. The pigs discover a crate of whisky in the farmhouse basement. "No animal shall drink alcohol" actually reads "No animal shall drink alcohol to excess,". Food grows ever scarcer, but Squealer continues to produce statistics to prove there is plenty of food. The sheep, chant "Four legs good, two legs bad!" **[4}**

1)

   a) NO CHANGE

   b) Squealer makes clear and explains that their leader

   c) Squealer explains that their leader

   d) Squealer elucidates and expounds that their leader

2)

   a) NO CHANGE

   b) affects

   c) effecting

   d) effect

3)

   a) NO CHANGE

   b) in the animals themselves. He commits to working even harder

   c) in the animals themselves, he commits to working even harder

   d) in the animals themselves; he commits to working even harder

4) The writer wants to insert the following sentence immediately after the last sentence in paragraph 3. Should the writer add this sentence?

The fault in the animals that Boxer had identified was that the animals couldn't see what was happening in front of their own eyes?

- a) Yes, because it is a concluding sentence for that paragraph.
- b) No, it only comments on Boxer.
- c) Yes, because it helps the reader.
- d) No, this just repeats what has already been stated.

In Act Three (page 52), Comrades! Loyalty and obedience are more important. One false step and our enemies will be upon us! Surely, comrades, you don't want Jones back!

5 In this extract, Squealer uses the idea of Jones' return most likely to:

- a) To imply that Jones is the only enemy.
- b) To infer a threat against disobedience.
- c) To imply that loyalty to Napoleon is most important.

In Act Three (page 55), Minimus reads out his latest poem. "Comrade Napoleon. Friend of the fatherless! Fountain of happiness! Lord of the swill-bucket! Oh, how my soul is on Fire when I gaze at thy Calm and commanding eye, Like the sun in the sky, Comrade Napoleon!

6 The writer's primary purpose in including the claim that Napoleon is, "Lord of the swill-bucket!" is:

   a) To highlight the absurdity of the claims in the poem.

   b) To identify Napoleon as a pig rather than another animal.

   c) To identify Napoleon as the leader of pigs.

In Act Three (pages 60-62), The Sheep change the chant. the focus shifts from the praise of Animal Farm, to praise of Animal Farm and Napoleon equally, to praise for Napoleon by himself.

7 This shift in focus is to illustrate:

   a) The increasing importance of Napoleon as the leader.

   b) Animal Farm's success is directly linked to Napoleon's leadership.

   c) a comparison of the growing cult of personality for Napoleon paralleling the cult of the personality for Stalin, in Russia.

In Act Three (Page 59) Boxer refers to the windmill, "It's nearly finished. I'm so proud."

8 In context to Boxer's character, how is the word, "proud" being used:

a) The word proud, in this context, reflects Boxer's pride in his own strength.

b) The word proud, in this context, reflects Boxer's delight in having nearly finished a project that will benefit all animals' lives on the farm.

c) The word proud, in this context, reflects Boxer's surprise that the windmill will soon be finished.

ACT FOUR

SAT QUESTIONS

Act 4: Brief Synopsis

Animal Farm is declared a republic, and Napoleon becomes president. .**{1}** One day, Boxer's strength fails; he collapses. Benjamin and Clover stay near their **[2]** friend, the pigs announce that they will arrange to bring Boxer to a human hospital, but when the cart arrives, Benjamin reads the writing and announces that Boxer is being sent to be slaughtered. **[3]** The animals begin panicking, they begin crying and shouted to Boxer that he must escape. They hear him kicking feebly inside the cart, but he is unable to get out.

Soon Squealer claims **[4]** to have been at the horse's side as he died—he says that Boxer died praising the glories of Animal Farm. Not long after the farmhouse receives a delivery from the grocer, and sounds of revelry erupt from within. All but Benjamin, Boxer's closest friend, know where the pigs found the money to buy another crate of whisky—it was up to Muriel the Goat to tell Benjamin the truth.

1)

    a) NO CHANGE.

    b) Boxer's strength fails, he collapses.

    c) Boxer's strength fails he collapses.

    d) Boxer's strength fails: he collapses.

2)

    a) NO CHANGE

    b) friend. The pigs

    c) friend; the pigs

    d) friend: the pigs

3)

    a) NO CHANGE

    b) The animals begin to panic; they are crying and shout after Boxer

    c) The animals begin panicking; they begin crying and shouting after Boxer

    d) The animals begin panicking; they begin to cry and shouted after Boxer

4)

    a) NO CHANGE

    b) will have been

    c) been

    d) have had been

In Act four (page 71), On Boxer's death Squealer claims he was with Boxer at the end. "I was at his bedside. He whispered in my ear. "Forward, comrades. Long live Animal Farm! Long live Comrade Napoleon! Napoleon is always right." Those were his very last words, comrades. "

5 Squealer's purpose is to:

   a) Comfort the animals with Boxer's last words.

   b) Use Boxer's death as a propaganda tool.

   c) Support the idea that Napoleon is always right.

ACT FIVE

SAT QUESTIONS

Act 5: Brief Synopsis

The farm [1] whom has grown richer, allows only the pigs and dogs to live comfortable lives. Squealer explains that the pigs and dogs do very important work—filling out forms and such- [2} this will give all animals opportunities to have a better life , but their lives go on very much as before. They never lose their sense of pride in Animal Farm and still fervently believe in the goals of the Rebellion—a world free from humans, with equality for all animals.

Clover summons the others hastily to the yard. There, the animals [3] gaze at amazement at Squealer walking toward them on his hind legs. Napoleon soon appears as well, walking upright; worse, he carries a whip. The sheep begin to chant, as if on cue: "Four legs good, two legs better!" The animals can no longer distinguish between the faces of pigs or humans.

Clover, whose eyes are failing in her old age, asks Benjamin to read the writing on the barn wall where the Seven Commandments were originally inscribed. Only [4] the last commandment remains "All animals are equal," However, it now carries an addition: "but some animals are more equal than others."

1)

    a) NO CHANGE

    b) that has

    c) which has

    d) who has

2)

    a) NO CHANGE

    b) this will give all animal's opportunities

    c) this will give all animal's opportunities'

    d) this will give all animals' opportunities'

3)

    a) NO CHANGE

    b) gaze of amazement

    c) gaze at amazement

    d) gaze in amazement

4)

    a) NO CHANGE

    b) the last commandment remains, "All animals are equal."

    c) last commandment remains; "all animals are equal."

    d) the last commandment remains all animals are equal.

In Act Five (page 92), the narrator tells us that Benjamin read the new commandment on the barn. "For once Benjamin consented to break his rule, and he read out to her what was written on the wall. There was nothing there now except one single Commandment.

ALL ANIMALS ARE EQUAL, BUT SOME ANIMALS ARE MORE EQUAL THAN OTHERS.

TEACHER ASSESSED WRITING OR DISCUSSION RESPONSE

ALL ANIMALS ARE EQUAL, BUT SOME ANIMALS ARE MORE EQUAL THAN OTHERS.

The new commandment is, of course, nonsensical and illogical. It is Orwell's famous paradox at the end of his novella.

Read Orwell's letter (George Orwell: Life in Letters), writes about his intentions for Animal Farm.

Of course, I intended it as a satire on the Russian revolution…I meant that that kind of revolution (violent, led by power-hungry people) can only lead to a change of masters not a change in the system. …The turning point of the story was supposed to be when the pigs kept the milk and apples for themselves. If the other animals had had the sense to put their foot down then, it would have been all right. … What I was trying to say was, "You can't have a revolution unless you make it for yourself; there is no such thing as a benevolent dictatorship.

Now read this criticism of Animal Farm

The characters in Animal Farm are as meaningful and deep as performing Circus animals with George Orwell as Ringmaster. Whatever Orwell was trying to say about the Russian Revolution he could have said it better in one of his newspaper or magazine articles.

Did Orwell succeed in his aim for Animal Farm, or do you agree with his critic who claimed that the characters in Animal Farm are, "…as deep and meaningful as performing circus animals with George Orwell as Ringmaster."

_____
_____
_____
_____
_____
_____
_____
_____
_____

'A' LEVEL QUESTIONS

'A' LEVEL ESSAY QUESTION TYPES

I. **In Act One**, Old Major is a hero, admired for his courage, dignity, and outstanding noble qualities. Discuss the character of Old Major in Act One and his impact on what follows.

II. **In Act Two**, there is a conflict between Snowball and Napoleon. Explain how this conflict may represent two different visions of society.

III. **In Act Three**, language becomes a political weapon. Consider how language is changed and used as propaganda up to the end of Act Three.

IV. **By the end of Act Four**, Boxer is presented to us as a victim deserving our sympathy. Consider this view and the alternative view that Boxer's fate was Boxer's fault.

V. Animal Farm provided George Orwell with an opportunity to present his pessimistic view that revolution inevitably becomes totalitarianism. How far would you agree/disagree and what evidence, in the play, supports your view?

How 'A' level essays are assessed and evaluated.

'A' level essays should be accurate, coherent and use appropriate terminology. The essay demonstrates a clear knowledge and understanding -thoughtfully personal rather than mechanical.

Band 1 responses do not move beyond a literal reading.

Band 2, evidence of engagement with some details, relevant concepts and mostly coherent.

Band 3, responses show a systematic, well-organized response that engages relevantly with key aspects of the passage.

Bands 4 and 5 responses are complete, confident, and increasingly sophisticated with analysis of meaning and technique.

1. Introduction

1. what you intend to analyze
2. background & authors intention.
3. relevant themes you will examine.
4. basic facts-unbiased voice

2. Thesis

1. your argument in response to the question,
2. Your interpretation of the question
3. a summary of what you intend to argue.

3. Each Paragraph

1. One point is supported with evidence (keep to thesis).
2. Evidence -quotations-descriptions
3. Move from observation to analysis (explain what your evidence means?)

4. **Conclusion**

    1. summarize your thesis
    2. how ideas agree or disagree with the question.
    3. be creative and inventive-offering your insight
    4. ensure ideas in the conclusion are not in the rest of the essay.
    5. Comment on if you think the text has been successful in doing what it was trying to do.

<u>Transitions</u>

- To understand/examine/explore X, we need to understand Y."

- Similarly, /Correspondingly-X equals Y

- By extension-X causes Y

- Another key factor is X plus X

- Not only - but also -X plus X

- Having said that- Y replaces X

- By contrast-X opposes X or offers an alternative Y

Printed in Dunstable, United Kingdom